The Butterfly Principle

André Hötzer

The Butterfly Principle

Bibliographical information of Deutsche Nationalbibliothek
[the German National Library]:
Deutsche Nationalbibliothek / the German National Library has recorded this publication in the Deutsche Nationalbibliografie [German National Bibliography]; detailed bibliographical data may be found online at http://dnb.dnb.de.
© 2017 André Hötzer
Typesetting, cover design, production and publishing by
BoD – Books on Demand
Illustrations by Daniela Henninger
ISBN: 978-3-7431-7077-3

Acknowledgements and thanks

It has taken me a whole lot longer to write this book than I had originally envisaged. I would like to thank all those who have helped me with this book. The book would not exist at all but for the support of many dear people who have helped me to bring it to completion.

First of all I must mention BoD – Books on Demand, with their sophisticated system that makes it possible for any author, even on a limited budget, to hold his book in his hands in printed form. Or one like me who calls on the full battery of professional support with all that this involves. Thanks to Dr. Bremer for her exceptionally generous support. I would also like to thank my proofreader, who brought a lot of sympathetic imagination to the task of correcting my very numerous errors, making it possible for the reader to have a fluent reading experience. My thanks too to the illustrator Daniela Henninger, who has succeeded in transforming my ideas into wonderful heart-warming pictures. Thanks to the entire team at BoD – you gave my book just the right final polish it needed.

And of course too my thanks go to my loved ones, my mother and my late father who made me the person that I am today. Especially to my mother Ursula, who has always believed in me. I am thankful too that I have the best children, Lisa, Nico and Jenni, that a father could ever wish for. And thanks to my longstanding partner and companion Monika whose understanding I can always count on. I love you all.

The following persons played a not inconsiderable part in the completion of this book: Sandra Mangano, Line Mangano, Hans Wiegand, Susanne Trösser and my sister Ursula Aldrian. They all read through my unfinished manuscript drafts repeatedly, with infinite patience, and corrected my mistakes – with the result that the book has gone on getting better and better. You gave me the benefit of your suggestions, and inspired me with courage in what has been one of my most exciting projects.

Many thanks for your friendship – it is only your help, and your special strengths, that have made this book possible.

Preface

What gives someone the idea of writing a book about bereavement?

The answer is quite simple: the older we get, the more frequently people are lost to us – through sickness, accidents or other blows of fate.

When this happens, what is the appropriate way of behaving towards the bereaved? How can we help them, advise them, inspire them with courage? What comforting words can we find for them and how do we find courage ourselves? And the most important thing – what do we say to children, when they lose a loved one to death? How can we give them security and support?

This book aims to help provide answers to these questions, and point out ways that are suitable for soothing pain and making it easier to deal with what has happened.

Perhaps, after reading this story, more than one person may come to see certain things in a different light.

I hope this book may succeed in helping people to draw on positive strength after such a severe loss as the death of a loved one.

André Hötzer

Table of Contents

Preface	7
The worst vacation ever	11
Marie talks to the light	16
"Do you know what death is like?"	24
The caterpillar and the butterfly	36
"Can you help Marie?"	45
I am the Light	51

The Butterfly Principle

The worst vacation ever

It's Sunday evening, the summer vacation is at an end. Next day school starts again for Marie. Like all children, the nine-year-old girl loves the vacation – but this has been the worst vacation she has ever known. The sun has already gone down. It seems as if for Marie it is never going to rise again.

Marie sits on her bed and cries. For days her tears have been flowing without stopping. Her misery is so great that she can't imagine ever being happy again after what has happened.

How can a child be expected to cope when even the grown-ups don't know how to deal with something of this kind? Marie is beginning to realize that no one can really help her to soothe the pain. Of course she has heard many comforting words in the last few days – but words of comfort cannot reverse what has happened. And the people who tried to comfort her are of course themselves deeply shaken, and it was often hard for them not to lose control. "Why?" asks Marie. "Why did it have to happen?" This pain just will not go away. What would have happened, she thinks, if I had been in the car with my parents? Might I perhaps have noticed the lunatic who was going far too fast and crashed into the car from behind, knocking it off the carriageway, in time for the accident to have been prevented?

Marie tries to sleep. Her eyes are burning, but her tears have dried up. And yet the pain is still there, deep down inside her. "How many times did I contradict Mom and Dad or not listen to them? Whereas now… I would do anything they asked me to. I would always be a good girl till the end of my life, if I could only wind back the clock. And perhaps then it would all turn out differently. Perhaps…"
Marie sighs deeply. "I would – yes, I would even be willing to die myself, if it could undo what has happened. Because then it wouldn't go on hurting so much. But that wouldn't help either, of course, because then Mom and Dad would have to suffer this unending pain." All kinds of questions dart through Marie's head, but she can't find any answers. "Is there no one who can help me? In normal situations the grown-ups always know what is the best thing to do – but now I am left completely alone with my anxiety and despair."

And just as Marie is so longing that someone would help her she suddenly has the feeling that she isn't alone in the room. It almost feels as if somebody is listening to her. "But I didn't say anything out loud – I was only mulling it over in my own head. So how could anyone know what I'm thinking? He would surely need to have telepathic abilities, and anyway apart from me there is nobody in the room."

But somehow she can't shake off the feeling that somebody is quite close nearby. It doesn't feel as unpleasant as it sometimes does, when she finds herself all alone in the room and gets anxious about ghosts or intruders – not to mention all the other reasons one dreams up for being terrified. This time it is definitely different, she doesn't feel scared. What she feels is actually quite calming.
Calm and reassurance – that is just what she needs.
But where does this warm feeling come from? Is she just imagining it? Just at the moment when she has this thought, she has the impression of a very gentle, warm breath stroking her cheek, almost like an angel touching her.

"That really feels nice, it's so lovely," Marie thinks.

It feels just like the times when her mother used to tuck her up in bed and read her a story. Always when she was very nearly asleep, her mother would stroke her cheek lovingly and then Marie could fall asleep without any worries. In remembering this, it occurs to her that her Mom is never going to do it any more, and she starts weeping bitterly again. She turns off the light and pulls the blanket over her head.
In spite of all the pain she is tired, worn out with weeping, exhausted with thinking. But her thoughts keep going round and round and her head rings, as if someone were hitting her on the head with a hammer.

"If only I could sleep, I would stop feeling the pain for the night at least." She thinks of the coming day. How is she possibly going to get through it? The other children are bound to know what has happened. After all, it was in the newspaper. Just how is Marie going to cope?
"I would rather not go to school at all. And what is the point, anyway?" she thinks.

As well as a headache she now has a stomach ache, probably because of the next day. But it could also be because she has hardly eaten anything for days. Her stomach refuses to take in food, because in the past she has always eaten with her Mom and Dad.

Now, since Uncle Nico took her in, he has done everything he can to get her to eat. Of course Uncle Nico also does what he can to comfort Marie, but he doesn't make a very good job of it. It's hard to comfort somebody when you are suffering yourself.

"Why did it have to be my brother and his wife?" Marie's uncle thinks. "Why them, of all people? They were what people see as a dream couple. Something that hardly exists any more in the ephemeral world of today. They had been married for ten years, and were still the dream couple. Actually dream couple isn't quite right, dream family would be more like it."
He knows that above all for Marie's sake he mustn't give up. "It is really strange, it always seems to happen to the wrong people. But just how can I help Marie?" For days he has been carrying around the idea of booking an appointment for Marie with a child psychologist.
"Yes," he finally decides. "They will know how to help her. First thing tomorrow, I'll make an appointment."

Marie talks to the light

Marie turns restlessly from side to side in her bed, she just can't fall asleep. First of all she can't stop thinking of her parents – and then she thinks too of this warm breath which so soothed her. That was the first time for days that she had felt anything resembling security.
"So there really is something that can soothe the pain," she thinks. But should she give way to this calming influence at all, should she even wish to be free of the pain?
On the one hand it's just what she longs for – but on the other, she is ashamed to stop thinking about her parents even for one second. It all makes for emotional turmoil.

"This feeling," she pleads, "please let me feel it again. Just for a brief moment I would like to be able to forget the pain."
Just as this thought goes through her head she again becomes aware of this breath, but this time it is stronger. It's almost as if someone were gently stroking her head. How she has been missing this feeling!

"Whatever can it be?" she asks in astonishment. "It feels so real, actually I should be frightened." And yet she isn't afraid. She pulls the blanket down and looks around the room which her uncle has given her in his house, but she can't make out anything, it's too dark.

She simply asks into the darkness: "Is somebody there?" She listens to the silence. "If somebody's there, please show yourself."

Suddenly she hears a warm, quiet voice speaking out of the darkness: "Yes, I am here."
Now Marie really does feel a bit queasy in the stomach. "Who are you?" she asks. "I am the light," comes back the answer.
"The light?" Marie asks in astonishment. "Is that the truth?"
"I am the light," whispers the voice again out of the darkness, without directly answering her question.

Now Marie feels uncertain whether she is really awake or is she just dreaming it all? She must be dreaming because surely this kind of thing only happens in dreams. But she doesn't really care too much whether she is asleep or awake – since how often, after all, do you get the chance of talking to a light?

"Hmm," Marie says thoughtfully, "if you are a light, why is it so dark in here?" "Well," responds the light, I didn't want to startle you."
"So does that mean that you can make yourself brighter?"
"Yes, as bright as you want," the light answers.
"Then please make yourself bright enough for me to see you!"

Hardly has Marie voiced this request when the room is filled with light. She can't see anything at all, it is so glaringly bright. It dazzles her and she has to hold her eyes tight shut as if she were looking directly into the sun.

"Can you turn down the brightness a bit?" Marie asks.
"Of course," says the light, and it becomes a little bit darker in the room.
"Is that better?" the light asks her.
The light now appears much smaller and does not beam so brightly – it's amazingly beautiful. Marie has never seen anything like it. It is so pure and so consoling, just what she was longing for.

"OK, even if it's only a dream, at least it's a nice dream," Marie thinks. She likes being in a dream conversing with a light.
"What do you want from me and how come you are here with me in my room?"
"Well," says the light, "I saw that you were so terribly sad and I wanted to be with you in order to comfort you. But it very rarely happens that anybody notices us at all."
"You said 'us' – does that mean that there are more lights like you?"
"Oh yes," the light answers. "We are all over the place but very few people perceive our presence. Mostly it's children who see us. It does sometimes happen that grown-ups notice us but usually they suppress the experience immediately, because they have been taught that something like us doesn't exist… can't possibly exist. What kind of reactions do you think a grown-up would provoke if he started telling people about us?"
"I understand," Marie answers. She has often had occasion to remark that grown-ups don't believe in things that are out of the ordinary.
"Did you stroke me?" she asks the light now.
"Yes, because you are unhappy."
"Yes, I am," Marie answers – " and I won't ever be happy again either, after what has happened."
"I know what happened," says the light. "And if you are sad that is absolutely OK. Only you mustn't let it hurt you too much because that

certainly isn't what your parents would have wanted for you. You know that they loved you very much?"

"Yes, and I loved them very much," answers Marie. "That's why I miss them so much, and it hurts that I won't ever see them again."

"Is that so?" asks the light.

"Of course, why do you ask such a question?" Marie replies.

"Well, how do you know that is the case?"

"What do you mean exactly?"

"How do you know that you won't ever see them again?" the light asks again.

Marie thinks about it. Yes, where does it come from, the certainty that she really never will see her parents again? How does she know that this is the case?

And with that thought she falls asleep.

"Marie, Marie, you must get up!" It's morning, and the voice is ringing in her ears. "Child, you must get up, or you'll be late for school!" she hears her Uncle Nico calling.

"Oh yes, school," Marie thinks. "Of course it's Monday, and the vacation is over."

Marie gets dressed and goes downstairs. She sits at the kitchen table and helps herself to the bread her uncle has buttered for her. She actually reaches out and helps herself to a slice of bread!

Her uncle sees this with approval and relief – it's the first time for days that his niece has shown any sign of recovering her appetite.

While Marie is eating, her thoughts go back to last night. That was such a strange dream. And she can't get that question of the light's out of her head: *How do you know that is the case?* Yes, where did she get this idea from actually? After all, this is a subject that is hardly ever talked about.

And up till now, Marie hasn't really asked anyone about it either. Perhaps she should ask Uncle Nico? But if he knew the answer, wouldn't he have said something about it to her long since? She can't make up her mind whether to ask him or not.

In the end she summons her courage, and asks, "Hey… Uncle Nico… – when a person dies, do we ever get to see them again?" Her uncle becomes white as a sheet – it wasn't a question he was expecting. He doesn't know whether he should lie to her in order to calm her down or whether he should tell her the truth. "But what is the truth?" he asks himself.

He swallows. Then he looks up inquiringly at the ceiling and doesn't utter a word. Now Marie feels almost sorry that she asked him. Her uncle doesn't look well at all – just as bleary-eyed as she does, and haggard, seeing that he too, since the accident, has been forgetting to eat and has lost a few pounds.

Uncle Nico says very quietly: "Marie… I don't know… I really don't know." He puts his arms around her and presses her hard to him as if he never wants to let her go.

They stay like that for quite a while, and when he lets go of her, she sees tears shining in his eyes. Then he says, "You know, Marie, I love you very much, and whenever you need me I will always be there for you."

Marie can see how seriously he means his promise. Then he adds: "Marie, as I don't know myself what would be the best way of helping you in this situation, I've made an appointment for you with a child therapist, a lady who talks to children, for Wednesday. She might have good advice for you and be better able to answer your questions."

Of course Uncle Nico has expressed himself in very objective fashion, but the fact is that he doesn't have anything to offer himself. He wants to be strong, though he feels altogether weak and helpless. He hugs Marie again and gives her a kiss on the forehead.
On her way to school Marie goes on thinking about all that has been happening to her.
When she enters the school playground, she sees many troubled faces. None of the children quite knows how to behave towards Marie. Perhaps a few of them have asked their parents whether they should try to comfort Marie, or whether it would be better not to refer to the death of her parents, so as not to remind her of what has happened.
But even the parents of those children were not sure. Some parents said to their children that it wasn't easy to give an answer, as they didn't know themselves what was best. Others again evaded their children's questions. And yet others said they should behave towards Marie in whatever way they thought proper.
Finally a few of the children come up to Marie and welcome her with a warm hug, and say nothing at all – just the hug says more than they could possibly express with a thousand words.

Sometimes it is good just to be there and to say nothing, and give the other person the feeling that you are with them in their pain.

"Do you know what death is like?"

In the lunch break, some of the children stand in a group and talk about Marie. One child says: "Poor Marie, I just can't imagine what it would be like without a Mom and Dad." The others nod in agreement.
When Marie goes to join the others to hang out with them, she wonders whether she should tell them about her meeting with the light last night. However she decides she had better keep it to herself. But what about her question? Her question whether she will ever see her parents again? And then there's another question, the question what is it like for them in the place where they are now? Is it all over or is there something after death?

Marie takes a deep breath, then she asks: "Do you know what death is like?"
The children exchange puzzled looks.
"What do you mean by that?" a boy asks.
"What I mean is, do we see the people we have lost ever again – are they all right, after they have left us? Can my parents see and hear me right now, can I talk to them? Or what happens after you are dead?"

These were questions that perhaps none of the children would have expected – though each of them had to admit, that they had often thought of these or similar questions and sometimes cried in the night, because they were afraid that their parents would die one day. Some were even in anguish over the thought that such a thing might happen to them soon. But none of them has a proper answer to Marie's questions. They just shrug their shoulders, though each of them wishes they knew the answer.

After school finishes, Marie goes home. She does her homework, has the evening meal with her uncle and goes to her room. The light is already fading. Marie goes to the window and looks out. Her uncle's house backs onto a wood. With the dark coming down she can only just distinguish the outline of the trees and the first stars are beginning to gleam in the sky. They look almost like the light in her dream, only much smaller. Marie looks at the stars and wonders whether it is possible that two of the stars might be her parents and they can see her now standing at the window.

Marie looks up and says: "Mom and Dad, I miss you such a lot and I love you SO very much."

Then she can't help crying. She puts on her pajamas and gets into bed. Just as she is getting into bed her uncle comes into the room like he does every evening. He sits on her bed and strokes her head. Of course he can see that she has been crying. He puts his arms around her and gives her a warm hug. She is glad that somebody is there to give her a hug. Before the accident it had always been been her mother or father doing it. Certainly it's not the same thing, but at least it gives her the feeling that she is looked after. That must be because Nico really does love her very much. Then he says: "Good night, little one."

As he is on the point of going out of the room Marie stops him and asks him the same question as before, which she just can't get out of her head: "Hey, Uncle Nico… don't you think it might actually be possible to see people we love who are gone some day again?"

This evening Nico is ready for Marie's question. No, he has decided, he won't tell her any lies, however much he loves her. Wouldn't she blame him for it later on, if he told her something he didn't really believe himself, just so as to appease her? Surely, after that, she would never be able to believe anything he said? No doubt about it. He wants to tell her the truth – he is a realist after all, and he knows that when a person dies you don't get to see them again.

A few years ago he himself lost his wife to a painful illness, and he hasn't seen her since – except in his dreams and in recollected pictures of the mind. This too is still painful for him, and he wonders constantly whether he might have been able to prevent it if he had urged her earlier to go to the doctor… And now, on top of that, he has to struggle with the loss of his brother and sister-in-law…

So he answers: "I'm terribly sorry that I have to say this to you, Marie, but you won't see them again – though you can always remember them and see them in your mind's eye the way you most like to see them."
"Why are you so sure of that?' Marie asks with disappointment, as if she would have preferred her uncle to lie to her.
"Because I've never seen anyone again after they have died," Nico answers – though he regrets it as soon as he has said it. "I know how you feel, Marie! And I am here for you." He strokes her head and goes out of the bedroom.

Marie is hit with a double dose of anguish, as now she knows the truth. If only she hadn't asked, then at least she would have been able to live in hope of one day seeing her parents again. Her eyes fill with tears once more. "Why, oh why should everything be over and done with for ever? I don't want it to be true – never, never, never!" she bursts out.

She beats her fists on the bed and weeps bitterly. At some point she falls asleep, still sobbing, and then she is woken by a warm peaceful voice, which says to her: "Don't be sad, little one, everything is going to be all right." Marie looks around the room and sees the little light again – it seems so friendly and comforting that Marie feels instantly better, just like at their first meeting, because the voice of the little light is like the voice of an angel.

"Hello, little light, I'm glad to see you again! Are your really here or am I just dreaming? Well, actually it doesn't matter – as long as you are with me, I feel better. Are you going to visit me every evening?" Marie asks. "As long as you want me to," answers the light. Marie looks at the light and asks, "Who are you? Are you real?" "I am as real as the air you breathe, Marie." "Are you a spirit?" Marie asks again.

"There are lots of names for me. Some people call me an angel or an apparition, others call me God, a fairy or a soul, and yet others just call me the light. Personally I find the last most attractive. I would like to bring light into the darkness," the light adds, "but you can decide for yourself what you would like to call me."

"I think light suits you best," Marie responds – "you are so beautiful, and when you are around I feel better, I feel looked after." Marie thinks she sees something like a smile in the light. Then she remembers what the light said to her before. *Don't be sad*, it said. "What did you mean when you said before that I shouldn't be sad because everything is going to be all right? Do you actually know something about death?" Marie asks the light. "Oh yes," the little light answers. "What would you like to know?"

Now, however, Marie feels a little bit uncertain, because she doesn't know whether it is a good idea to ask yet again the question she is so concerned about – for how would it be if she doesn't get the answer she hopes for from the light either? What if she gets the same answer that she had from Uncle Nico? Might it be better not to ask after all, so as to go on living with the hope of seeing her parents again one day?

The little light notices that Marie is hesitating. "You needn't be afraid to ask your questions," it reassures Marie. Marie notices that her fear is gradually diminishing – she feels so good when the light is close to her. The light radiates such a pleasant warmth.

"I guess that's how a baby feels in its mother's tummy," Marie thinks. She summons all her courage and asks the light: "Do you know what is happening to my mother and my father, will I ever see them again? Where are they now, are they all right?" The little light answers in calm tones: "You know, Marie, what you call death is not the end."

"If it's true what you say, why I am having such a bad time and why are most people afraid of death?" Marie asks the light in a quiet voice.

"This is because from time immemorial there have been people who tried to make other people terrified of death. These people practically blackmailed the rest, and told them that if they didn't do this, that or the other, they would go to hell, where they would suffer a thousand torments and disappear forever into the darkness. But if they did what they were told by the blackmailers, then they would be spared suffering after death. This had the result that people became afraid – afraid to do something wrong, afraid of saying the wrong thing or just afraid of death. Of course it was all lies, but people were so frightened that they did everything that was expected of them…"

The light stops for a moment, and then says: "Just imagine this. What's it like, if you and a blind man are standing in front of a gorgeous field of poppies? The blind man can't see the field – so does the field exist or does it not? True or false? Just because he doesn't *see* it, does that mean the field doesn't exist? Or perhaps he can smell it and feel it? But suppose he can't do that either?"

Does that mean that the field isn't there?" "Of course not," Marie replies, "the field is there all the same, even if he can't see or feel it." "That's right, Marie, that's just how it is." Then the light continues: "Let's suppose that you could determine how your parents are doing and where they are right now, what would you choose for them?"

Little Marie thinks for a moment, looks at the light and answers: "I know what I would wish, but that is just my wish, isn't it – and I would really like to know how my parents are actually doing." "Well, Marie, just imagine this. Suppose it were possible to decide how dead people get on when they are dead or where they go to. You see, there are lots of possibilities. Let's suppose every person who has died will be re-born, somewhere in this world. Or we can imagine they become an angel and protect all those they are particularly fond of. It is also possible that the same life replays again from the beginning, or that people come back again as animals. Perhaps they might even become a light like me, or a beautifully shining star in the heavens. Perhaps too they could be quite close to you, only you can't see them. What I am trying to say is that it is up to you how your parents are getting on, and what place you want them to be in for you. If you want them to be two bright stars in the sky, and to give you help and advice when you need it, that is what they will do. If you would like to talk to them you only have to call their names and you can be certain that they will answer."

Marie is a bit confused. She looks at the light and asks: "How do you mean? Does that mean if I want my parents to be having a good time, then that is the way it is?' "Yes", answers the light, "exactly like that. It is actually quite simple."
Marie considers, and then something occurs to her. Once her Mom said to her that when she was gone, Marie only had to look up into the sky.

There among the most beautiful stars in the sky, that is where she would find her. She hadn't understood it at the time but now her mother's words make some kind of sense.

"You've got it," says the light.

"But why should people have to die at all?" Marie asks.

"People die only when they have accomplished their task on earth. That is, they are with us on the path for a certain time, and when we don't need them any longer, they are given a different task and so death is not the end, it is rather the beginning of something new. Most people are only afraid of death because they don't know what comes afterwards. Actually it is very unreasonable to suppose that death is the end, for who (apart from me, and now you as well) knows for sure what happens when we die? Since we both know now that we have a choice – that we can decide for ourselves how life is to go on after death."

"How come you know all this?" Marie asks.

"Well, I was once a human being and I too was afraid of death, and I thought that when I came to die I would like to become a light. A light that drives away the darkness, a light that helps other people conquer their fear of death. And now here I am with you! It has to be said that I can only visit people who summon me as you did when you asked: *Is there no one who can help me*? When I sensed that you needed my help I came to you – and in the same way I can help other people to get over their fear of death. Anybody can see and sense us, they only have to let it happen. The problem with grown-ups is that they only believe what can be proved. They want to see everything with their own eyes, and not with the heart. People often feel that someone is close to them, and then they get goosebumps or a pleasantly warm feeling, they hear a sound and don't know where it is coming from. It's coming from us, and we are just there to show them that they don't need to be afraid and they are not alone. And what do the grown-ups do? They look for an explanation for anything that is out of the ordinary – they persuade themselves that perhaps a window has been left open, the floor is creaking or it was just the wind blowing something around. They always want to think logically, you see. And as a result, they leave out the most important thing. It happens from time to time, that a grown-up calls me and we talk for quite a while and then suddenly – in the middle of the conversation – he breaks off. Do you know why that happens, Marie? The person suddenly has doubts. They suddenly ask themselves who they are talking to. Whether they can trust their senses or whether they are just imagining it all and talking to themselves. They get doubts! They think: *Who could I tell about this? People would think I was crazy.* And yet the truth is, they don't have to tell anybody about it. Because in the end, the only thing that matters is that they are better off when I am with them."

"But I don't see that now," Marie says. "Surely it would be a whole lot better if people would talk about such things, then much fewer people would be afraid of death."
"That is true," responds the light, "of course it would be better. And perhaps you are the one, little Marie, who can help other people in this way, by helping them to lose their fear of death."
Marie thinks, and then says: "Hey... little light... in my class there are some children who are afraid of death too, or they are afraid that something might happen to their parents one day. I could tell them about our talk, I suppose?"

"That's a really good idea, Marie, because children specially don't have any fixed ideas about death. They only learn that death is a bad thing when they are older. If we both believe it and you talk to your friends at school about it, and they talk to their friends, and they talk to their parents and the parents talk to the neighbors, then at some point all the people of the world will lose their fear of death."

Marie ponders for a while and then asks the light: "I say… do you think it would be a good idea to talk to my uncle about it? You know, it might do him some good as well."
"That is a very good idea," says the light encouragingly.
"First thing tomorrow, I'll talk to my uncle about it," Marie resolves.
"OK – but now you had better get some sleep, little Marie – I'll stay with you until you fall asleep," the light whispers.

The caterpillar and the butterfly

Next morning, after Marie has got dressed, she goes straight away to her Uncle and tells him what has happened to her the last two nights. She tells him about the light and all the things the light has shared with her, and she also tells him about the story of the blind man in the field.

When Uncle Nico hears what Marie tells him he finds it hard to think clearly – on the one hand he is glad that Marie is happier, on the other it is clear to him that she is getting a bit carried away with it all and he is afraid this might lead to a painful disappointment later on. When she is older, if not before, she will realize that death really is the end of everything and he would like to spare her that at any price.

He realizes that he is pushing his limits here because he simply has no idea what to say to Marie in response to her story. Perhaps he should just say nothing at all and leave it to the therapist. Perhaps the therapist will be better able to help Marie to cope with the situation.
He says to Marie: "It's all very interesting what you are telling me. Do you think you could tell the therapist about it tomorrow?"
"Of course," says Marie. Then she asks him: "What does a therapist do actually?" "She helps you find answers to questions you are interested in," answers Nico. Marie thinks about it. She can see that her uncle is concerned that she should meet the therapist.

On her way to school Marie wonders whether she should tell anyone in her class about her experience with the light.

Finally she decides that to begin with she will just tell her best friend Lisa about it, in order to see how she reacts. She is already a little bit afraid that the others might laugh at her.
In the lunch break she joins her friend Lisa on a bench. Marie gives her an account of her meetings with the light and the conversations they have had. She tells her how she has learned that people don't actually go away for ever when they die, they only turn into something different. Her friend Lisa is not at all inclined to laugh at Marie's revelation – she even finds it all quite exciting.

Lisa says thoughtfully: "You know, that's kind of the way it was with the caterpillar and the butterfly."
And then Lisa tells Marie about an experience she had when she was a little girl. She had found a caterpillar and brought it home. Then she was away for a few days with her parents, so she put the caterpillar in the front garden. But what a shock she had when she got back! The caterpillar was dead, only its shriveled husk was left hanging on the branch. Lisa goes on to say that she was terribly sad at the time about the death of the caterpillar, but then her mother came to her and said, "Lisa, you don't have to be sad, the caterpillar isn't dead, it has only been transformed – it has turned into a beautiful butterfly!"

"Well, that is a nice picture," Marie replies to her best friend Lisa.

Next day Marie drives with her uncle to the therapist, who has her practice a little way out of town. When they arrive and get out of the car, Marie is looking at a beautiful old villa. The villa looks very friendly, and somehow as if it has a sense of humor as well – it is painted pink, and has white window frames and blue shutters. It looks like a very old house.

"I wonder if the therapist is nice?" Marie thinks.

Uncle Nico asks Marie to wait just a moment in the front garden. He wants first to have a talk with the therapist on his own, and tell her what Marie told him yesterday morning and how he has been very concerned about it. The therapist listens to Nico attentively. When he has finished his story and falls silent she takes his hands in hers, gives him a reassuring look and promises him: "Don't worry, I will help Marie, she is going to be all right soon. Best thing would be if you go for a walk for a couple of hours and then we will see how we are getting on."
When her uncle emerges from the villa again, Marie sees that he is frowning. But then he smiles at Marie and says: "It's OK, Marie, we can go in now."
When they enter the beautiful hall of the villa Marie observes that the house is just as friendly inside as it looked from the outside.

A moment later, Marie and her uncle are standing at a large, snow-white wooden door. When her uncle knocks on the door she hears a friendly voice calling from inside: "Please come in!" As the two of them enter the room Marie looks at the therapist with curiosity. She is quite small and has gray wavy hair. "Somehow she looks so wise and she really goes with this house," thinks Marie.

With a smile on her face the therapist comes to meet Marie and welcomes her: "Hello, Marie, I am called Ursula, and I would like to have a bit of a talk with you. Would it be OK for you if your uncle has a chance to recover from the drive and goes out for a little walk?" Marie thinks for a moment, looks at the old lady and senses that she can trust her. "Yes, that's fine," she answers.

Marie and Ursula go into a small cozy room. It offers a great view of the beautiful park at the back of the house. "If you like, we can sit outside on the terrace," says Ursula.

"That would be nice," Marie replies.

"Would you like a tea or would you rather have something cold?" Ursula asks Marie.

"I would like a cold drink, please," Marie answers.

"Fine, just sit down at the table out there and I'll get us something."

As Marie is waiting she looks around the park for a bit. On one branch she sees a few caterpillars which are just on the point of pupating. That really is strange. Hadn't she just been talking to her friend Lisa about it?

Just as she makes the connection an amazingly beautiful butterfly lands right on Marie's shoulder. This butterfly looks really magical and seems not to be afraid of the girl at all – and before she notices it, a second butterfly lands right on her hand.

"Oh, I say, that is nice," says Ursula, coming out onto the terrace with the tray, "you've already made friends with my favorite butterflies. Now here's a delicious iced tea with ice cubes for you and a hot tea for me… you can see, it's just steaming away." She emphasizes this as if she were trying to tell Marie something.

Ursula settles down in her favorite armchair, then she continues her talk with Marie. "Your uncle has told me what happened. He thought it would most probably be a good thing if you were to talk to somebody who has had a lot of experience about it all. What do you think?"

Marie thinks for a moment, wondering what she should tell Ursula. Would it be a good idea to talk to her about the light? "I don't have any idea just what to say," she begins hesitantly.

"Just say anything, whatever is going through your head right now," says Ursula.

Marie starts by telling Ursula about her parents' accident. About the pain which she thinks is never going to go away. Then she tells her how her uncle has taken her to live with him. She admits that in spite of her uncle's care she has been in a bad way – she has lost her appetite and she was reluctant to go to school.

Ursula listens carefully and takes a sip of her tea.

Marie is uncertain whether she should tell Ursula about the light as well. While she is pondering this a sunbeam shines directly through the tree tops onto Ursula's hair. Her whole head becomes dazzling, making the therapist look ever so much nicer. Thereupon Marie plucks up courage and tells Ursula about her encounter with the light. Finally she comes to the end of her story and asks Ursula: "And what do you think about it – did I just dream it all, or am I just imagining it?"

Ursula looks at Marie with understanding and smiles.
"You know, Marie, there are many things that we don't understand or can't explain and yet they exist. There are certain notes that we humans can't hear and yet they are there. The same goes for light, there is visible and invisible light – just because we can't see it that doesn't mean that it doesn't exist. So why shouldn't your light exist too?"

"And what do you think of what the light told me about death?"

"Well, I think it is the way the light explained to you. Just take a look at our drinks and what do you see?"

"Tea," answers Marie, though she thinks to herself, "Now that really is a funny question."

"Correct," Ursula agrees, "but didn't your glass also hold an ice cube a moment ago?"

"That's right", answers Marie. "You see, ice becomes water, and when I bring water to the boil, to make my tea, it becomes water vapor. That doesn't mean that the water no longer exists, it just means that it has changed its form. In the end it is the same as with the caterpillar and the butterfly."

Marie looks at Ursula, who is still lit up with the sun's rays. The brightness reminds her rather of the little light who visits her every evening.

Marie says: "Does that mean that my parents are OK?" "That's right," Marie." "And I can talk to them whenever I want to?" "That's right too." This is something Marie would never have expected at all, that a grown-up would actually believe her.

That is comforting, to know that her parents are OK. Of course it would be much nicer if they were still around, but the thought that she can talk to them whenever she likes and ask their advice does make her feel easier.

Her thoughts are interrupted by the doorbell. A moment later there is Uncle Nico once again. The two hours seem to have gone by in no time at all.

Uncle Nico asks Marie if he could just have another quick chat with Ursula alone. Marie says that is all right. She hopes that Ursula may be able to help her uncle as well.

"Can you help Marie?"

"Well?" Nico asks Ursula. "What have you got to tell me, how did the talk go and can you help Marie?"
"I find it very exciting and remarkable what Marie tells me about death and her meeting with the light. You know, it is often the case that children intuitively know a whole lot more than adults. This is because they have not yet lost the ability to see with the heart. And sometimes it is a good thing to take something of their point of view on board."

This answer is one Uncle Nico really had not expected. "What are you trying to say?" he asks again. "Do you actually believe this stuff Marie has been telling you?"

"Let me just explain it to you like this," Ursula replies. "You know what kind of thing plants and trees can turn into?" "Of course I know," Nico answers. "But I don't see what that has to do with Marie." "Well, you'll find out in a moment if you just tell me what kind of thing plants can turn into."

Nico starts to enumerate: "Well, we get wood from a tree, and wood can be made into furniture, and you can use wood to make a fire, and it is also useful for making paper. And then timber and plant residue can be made into fertilizer, coal, oil, gas and even diamonds." "That is all quite correct," says Ursula with an affirmative nod. And then she adds: "Sand turns into glass. Ice into water, water turns into water vapor. A caterpillar becomes a butterfly. Do you agree with me so far?"

"Yes, you are right," Nico answers. "But I still don't understand what this has to do with Marie."

"Do you agree with me that everything can change its form and its state?" Ursula asks. "Yes, I can agree with that," Uncle Nico replies.

"So if it is the case that this applies to everything in the world, why should it not apply to us human beings as well? When we human beings die we too just change our state, we are transformed. Just because we don't see or grasp something, that doesn't mean that it isn't happening. In former times people believed that the earth was a disk and at the end of the horizon you would fall over the edge. The earth did not then suddenly become round overnight just because people found you could keep going beyond the horizon – on the contrary, it had always been round, people just weren't in a position to prove it. Perhaps some day we will be in a position to prove that there is life after death. But to suppose, just on the grounds that we can't prove it, that it is not the case would be just like denying that the caterpillar turns into a butterfly. What do you think the blind man would say if he were to find the empty husk of the caterpillar and you were to tell him: *Don't worry, the caterpillar is not dead, it has just been transformed into a beautiful butterfly*? He could either believe you or refuse to be convinced. And if you ask my opinion, I find the idea of a life after death much pleasanter than the idea that death is the end of everything. Which would you rather have?" Ursula asks Uncle Nico again.

"Of course, if we could choose for ourselves I guess everyone would want there to be some kind of continuing existence after death," he answers.

"That's it," Ursula concurs, "and whether or not you believe it, is entirely up to you. Perhaps you may find this little parable helpful, as it was once told to me." And Ursula starts to tell a story.

A very long time ago, in a distant country, there lived on a mountain a wise old man of whom people said that he knew everything. Two brothers got the idea of asking the old man a question that he wouldn't be able to answer. For hours they sat in a meadow trying to think what question they should put to the old man. One of them climbed up a tree, to be able to think better. On a branch alongside him he saw a little bird that was twittering quietly to itself. All of a sudden he seized the bird and held it firmly grasped in his hand. When he came down to his brother he called out: "I've got it! I know what we're going to ask the old man." He showed his brother the bird in his hand and said: "I will ask him whether the bird in my hand is dead or alive! And if he says the bird is alive I will squeeze it to death with my hands. But if he says that the bird is dead I will let it fly away!"

They ran excitedly up the mountain to the hut of the old man. He was sitting meditating at the front of his dwelling. Before they came near, the brothers called out: "Old man, we're going to ask you a question that you definitely won't be able to answer!" The two lads finally stood panting in front of the wise man. After a while he slowly opened his eyes and looked at the brothers. "Old man, we've got a question for you!" repeated one of the brothers. "Then ask it," answered the old man.

The brother with the bird in his hand looked at the old man, sure of victory, and asked, "All right, then. Wise man, in my hand is a bird, and I would like to hear you tell me whether the bird is dead or is it alive?"

The brothers gazed fixedly at the old man. He closed his eyes, thought for a moment, opened them again and then said: "My son – whether the bird is dead or alive is entirely in your hands." (Anonymous)

"And as for what concerns Marie," said the therapist, resuming her conversation with Nico, "she feels very comfortable with the thought of life after death – do you want to take this idea away from her, as it has been taken away from you? You should think again, and think deeply, about our conversation and above all about your talk with Marie. There are a great many people who can see and yet are blind to the most important thing."

Nico is perplexed. When he leaves the old house with Marie he has more questions whirring through his head than before the visit to the therapist. Actually he had expected something quite different to emerge from their visit.

On the drive home, he remembers a talk he had with his father many years ago. His father said to him at the time that every person relies on his or her own experiences in forming an opinion. If they have new experiences and acquire new information, this can form the basis for changing their point of view. So that means that we all have the choice to decide what we want to believe in.
When the two of them get home it is already very late. After this exciting day, Uncle Nico puts Marie to bed and sits down on the bedside. Marie looks at her uncle and says with relief: "Thank you for driving to Ursula's with me. It was really nice. I could talk about all my questions with her." "I was glad to do it. You know, Marie, you really are something quite special, and I love you very, very much." He gives her a kiss on the forehead and then goes to his office in the basement. This is the place he always goes when he wants to think about something quietly.

He sits down at the desk and recapitulates what Ursula said to him. "Was that just a therapeutic trick?" he asks himself. "Was she just wanting to comfort Marie with her parables so that she would be better able to cope with the situation? Or was her main aim to stop me from worrying? What did she mean with her talk about the transformation of all kinds of things? Don't therapists have to be rational in their approach to a problem and tell one the truth in all cases? But what if it actually is true, and we are not in a position to see or prove that there is life after death, just as once upon a time it wasn't possible to prove that the earth was round and not a disk?" What was that story again? What had Marie said to him about the blind man?

"That's right," Nico reflects, "the blind man can't see the field but he can hear the wind that wafts over the field, he can smell the scent given off by the poppies, he can taste a blade of grass and feel the grass under his feet."
And Ursula had said to him: *Just because we can't perceive or explain something, that doesn't mean that the thing does not exist.*
Could it actually be possible that there is a form of existence after death? Could it be the case that he can get in touch with his wife and his brother, that he can speak to them? Is it possible that they are close to him right now?

Just at the moment when he has this thought, for a brief second he has the feeling that the room has become a bit brighter and warmer. It is an agreeable warmth. And at the same time he feels a light, warm current of air, almost as though an angel were stroking his cheek in gentle agreement.

The End

I am the Light

I am the Light.
I am not dead, believe me, for I am with you always.
Do not weep over my grave, I am not there, I am not gone.
I am always here, I am with you.
I am the day and the night too, I am the one who watches over you.
I am the wind on your face, the foam on the sea.
Gaze into the darkness of night, I am the glittering of the stars.
I am the shiver you feel when the thought of me touches you.
I am the smile when you think of me, the air you breathe when you run.
I am the scent of the rose as you know it.
Never will I leave you. I am there when you need me, have no fear.
Do not stand over my grave and mourn, I am not there, I am not gone.
I am present everywhere. In the day I am the sunlight, by night I am the brightest star.
I am the rustling of the trees and the one who haunts your dreams.
I am the wind, the child of heaven.
I am the scent of the wood that bewitches you, as you once bewitched me.
As the winter snow is not really gone, when it transforms to rain –
So I too remain and am not gone – I wish to abide in your heart, that is the best home.
I am not gone, I am always there and neither time nor space can divide us, that is the truth.

Now a small caterpillar no longer, I am the most beautiful butterfly in the garden – just wait till I come and stroke you, as you once stroked me.

Where there is shadow, there is light – you may not see me but you can feel my presence, for I am not dead, I am life, and whenever you want I will guide you.

You belong to me as I to you, I am a part of you as you of me.

If you wish, you can see me – for remember the person may depart, but the soul never dies.

André Hötzer

If I knew that it was to be the last time I would see you going to sleep, I would tuck you in better and pray to God to protect your soul.

If I knew that it was to be the last time I would see you going out the door, I would hug you and kiss you and call you back for another kiss.

If I knew that it was to be the last chance I would have to say "I love you", I would say it, rather than assuming that you know that I love you.

There must always be a "tomorrow" if it is to be possible for an "oversight / error" to be cleared up.

There will always be another day on which to say "I love you", and there will undoubtedly be another chance of saying, "Can I do anything for you?"

But just in case I might be wrong I would like to say to you how much I love you – "tomorrow" is not promised to anybody and today could be the last chance that you have to hold your loved ones close to you.

So if you are waiting for tomorrow why don't you act today?
If "tomorrow" never comes you will certainly regret that you didn't have time for a smile, a hug or a kiss and that you were too preoccupied to admit something to somebody.

Hold your loved ones close to you today, and whisper in their ear – tell them how very much you love them and that you always will love them, find time to tell them: "I'm sorry," "Please forgive me," "Thank you" or "It's all right."

"… and if there proves to be no "tomorrow"… you won't have to regret today." (Anonymous)